CHOOSING AN ABUNDANT MINDSET

FOR EMOTIONAL TRANQUILTY AND WHOLENESS

CHOOSING AN ABUNDANT

MINDSET

G.P MARIANO STEFANI

Book Contents

Introduction

CONGRATULATIONS ON purchasing **CHOOSING AN ABUNDANT MINDSET: FOR EMOTIONAL TRANQUILTY AND WHOLENESS** and thank you for doing so. The following chapters will discuss where most anxiety, stress, and depression come from and how to beat it with natural tricks.

Chapters will also discuss how this stressful lifestyle affects your overall health, and how putting simple habits in place will help you overcome it. You'll learn how to distinguish anxiety from legitimate worry, and how to put an end to the constant worrying. The goal of this book is to give you the tools you need to start living life and stop spending all of your time worrying.

Excessive worrying leads to debilitating anxiety and depression. Worrying about the potential outcomes of every situation, every decision can be extremely stressful. This affects not only your ability to live a full life but your physical health as well. It can also affect not just your own quality of life, but the quality of life of your family and children.

When you are constantly worried, you tend to hesitate or avoid making decisions of any kind. It can stop you from doing the things you want to do for your career, your family, or your general happiness. This book aims to teach you ways to eliminate your worries and fears so that you can move forward with a much more productive life.

This book will teach you seven habits that you can start practicing right away to stop worrying and eliminate anxiety, stress, and depression. These seven habits may seem simple in concept, hard to put into practice. But over time these seven simple things will lead you to a much happier, more fulfilling life.

There are plenty of books on this subject on the market, thanks again for choosing this one! Every effort was made to ensure it is full of as much useful information as possible, please enjoy!

Chapter 1:

Understanding Anxiety, Stress, and Depression

In this chapter, we are going to be taking a closer look at what anxiety stress and depression are. We will be defining each term in addition to providing some insight into each condition. When most people hear either one of these terms, they imagine some individual who can't keep it together.

WORRYING ABOUT A LOT of different things all of the time is the beginning of a vicious cycle. It is natural to worry at certain times or in certain situations. But if you find yourself worrying about many things each day, you could be putting yourself at risk for severe depression.

Worry about day to day activities and the details of life, in general, can lead to debilitating anxiety. Anxiety is more than just worry. Anxiety has very real physical effects. You may find your heart racing, your blood pressure elevated, and you may feel dizzy as a result. You could even experience chest pain.

Anxiety can make you freeze up, feeling as though you are incapable of thought or action. Anxiety is extremely stressful. Stress has a different effect on everyone, but there are some definite effects of stress that have been recorded in various studies. Stress can make you feel overly tired. It can make you eat more or not at all, causing problems with fluctuating blood sugar. It can also cause you to gain weight over time as your body stores fat due to cortisol, the stress hormone.

Stress can be extremely overwhelming. Combined with anxiety it often leads to inaction, the inability to take any action in any situation. The more stressed you become, the more likely it is that you will forgo doing things you enjoy, or that you will forgo doing things that need to be done. This feeling of being overwhelmed often leads to depression, which can become severe over time.

You begin to feel lost in a sea of your own inadequacy. Because you cannot stop worrying and stressing about life, your mind creates a trap for itself preventing you from living it. Not living your life makes you feel as though you are letting down yourself and everyone around you.

Depression has its own effects on physical and mental health. You may find yourself sleeping much more than usual. This is your mind's escape from the depressed reality it is living in. On the other hand, some people with depression find that they cannot sleep when they should. They feel tired all day but stay awake, and then in the evening cannot settle their minds to sleep.

Depression can lead to binge eating or a complete lack of appetite. It can lead to fast weight changes, either a gain or loss depending on how your appetite reacts to the hormones. Over time this can have a serious impact on your health. Most importantly, depression keeps you inactive and prevents you from taking joy in the smallest things in life. And, of course, if you are depressed, you are spending a lot of your time thinking about how you got to that point. You begin worrying about all of the things you're not doing because of your depression. This simply starts the cycle over again and leads to higher anxiety, more stress, and a deeper depression. It is a vicious cycle that can seem never-ending.

The Science

THERE IS ACTUALLY SCIENCE that backs up the cycle of anxiety, stress, and depression. These effects are not "imaginary" or "all in your head." As you worry about the details of life, the chemistry of your brain actually changes. This makes the effects of anxiety and depression actual physical problems. The three neurotransmitters that affect mood are serotonin, dopamine, and epinephrine. A deficiency in any of these neurotransmitters can lead to clinical depression. A deficiency in serotonin is also typically linked with physical manifestations of anxiety disorders.

When you worry you become stressed. This stress releases a hormone into the body called cortisol. An excess of cortisol can decrease metabolism and affect the levels of serotonin and dopamine in your brain. As serotonin levels decrease your sense of well-being also decreases, leading to anxiety. As your anxiety increases, and stress becomes overwhelming, dopamine levels can also decrease. When a dopamine deficiency is present, clinical depression comes into play.

The problem with all of this is that it is a physical manifestation of the same emotional cycle already discussed. As dopamine and serotonin levels decrease, stress becomes higher and more cortisol is produced. The more cortisol that is produced, the lower your neurotransmitters are produced. The cycle can seem never-ending.

Medication

SOME PEOPLE TURN TO medications to help them cope with their anxiety and depression. These can be helpful while learning to break the mental and emotional cycle of worry, anxiety, stress, and depression. However, they should not be looked upon as a permanent fix. Anxiety medications increase serotonin levels and decrease epinephrine, making you feel less worried and stressed while also decreasing the flight response. Anti-depressants increase serotonin and dopamine production so that your brain is tricked into thinking that everything is okay, even if your thoughts are telling it otherwise.

Anti-depressants can make it easier to function and will combat the scientific reason for your depression. While medications can be helpful in combating the symptoms of anxiety and depression, it is unwise to rely on them solely. If you do not want to take these medications long term, you will have to learn how to control your anxiety, stress, and depression on your own through building healthy habits to control worry and stress. The following chapters of this book will help you take the first steps toward controlling your worrisome thoughts to help you better cope so that you don't have to rely on medications for your well-being.

Hollywood films and television shows often depict depressed people as folks who are on the verge of suicide. And while untreated depression does lead to thoughts of suicide, that is not always the case. Also, anxiety is depicted as an unbearable feeling which leads sufferers to go through all kinds of unbearable situations such as lack of sleep, or uncontrollable shaking. Of course, both of these conditions do have some of those symptoms associated with them; they are often prevalent in perfectly healthy people.

These are folks who seemingly have everything together in life, but inside, are struggling with these conditions.

Other times, anxiety and depression get a hold of highly successful people
who seem to have everything figured out. They are great at what they do, earn a decent living and are even the life of the party. However, they are struggling to keep their heads above water.

Then, some folks can't function anymore. These conditions have overrun them to a point where they cannot function as a regular person would. They cannot control their feelings to a point where even basic, daily activities can prove to become overwhelming. But what is anxiety? Anxiety is that uncontrollable, unshakable feeling of worry and concern about the future, what might happen or about things which are currently happening.

Sure, it's natural for everyone to feel nervous and anxious from time to time. Think about truly stressful situations such as taking a big test, or having to speak in front of a large audience. These are examples of situations which can cause anyone to lose sleep or even tremble with anticipation.

However, when the stressful situation is gone, then the person will be able to return to their normal condition. The stressful reaction dissipates and life goes back to normal. For those who suffer from anxiety, life doesn't go back to normal. That's because there is no normal. There is only worry and anguish.

This can lead the sufferer to lose sleep, become irritable and even experience physical symptoms such as digestive distress, skin rashes or overeating. Thus, anxiety is generally a reaction to a stressful situation. Consequently, stress is the most important cause of anxiety though not the only one. While we will get into the causes of stress in a later chapter, it's worth noting that stress, or a stressful situation, will generally be the precursor to anxiety.

Often, the symptoms of anxiety are so mild that even the sufferer will have a hard time picking them up. These symptoms are often dismissed at just regular stress derived from working too much or having too many things to worry about. Over time, stress builds up. Stress can build up to a point where the sufferer begins to manifest a condition called "burnout." In modern medicine, "burnout" is seen as a point in which the mind and body can no longer cope with chronic stress. Burnout is seen when the sufferer simply shuts down and

begins to exhibit serious physical health concerns. Nevertheless, burnout is just one physical manifestation of stress and anxiety. Since anxiety is predominantly mental and emotional, some sufferers may only present mild physical symptoms despite being emotionally distraught.

Fortunately, burnout can be treated with a combination of rest and medication. Anxiety, on the other hand, requires a much broader treatment, which may include medication, but almost always implies therapy. For some folks, their anxiety is just a condition they must live with for the rest of their lives and medication only helps alleviate the symptoms.

As for depression, this is, by far, one of the most debilitating mental and emotional conditions. Depression usually sets in as a result of chronic stress and/or untreated anxiety. For some folks, anxiety and depression work in tandem. For others, untreated anxiety leads to depression. Either way, depression can virtually destroy a person's life. As with anxiety, depression sufferers aren't necessarily in bed all day wallowing about whatever it is that has caused these feelings. In fact, some of the most successful individuals you might meet are living with a condition known as "high functioning depression." This type of depression is virtually impossible to detect as the sufferer does not exhibit some of the most traditional symptoms such as sadness and suicidal thoughts.

So, depression can be defined as extreme feelings of despondency and dejection. In short, depression is about feeling like there is nothing worth living for. It feels that life is not worth it anymore. When untreated, depression can lead to thought of suicide. And often, sufferers will act upon those thoughts if they do not receive the treatment they need. Medically speaking, depression can be treated through a combination of medication and therapy. Upon diagnosis, a doctor may prescribe antidepressants and therapy. This combination usually leads to positive results though some depression sufferers may end up taking medication for the rest of their lives. However, prolonged exposure to antidepressants has serious side effects. So, this is why it is critical to address the root causes of the depression. As I stated earlier, the symptoms of both anxiety and depression might be virtually undetectable. Nevertheless, there are warning signs which you need to keep an eye on. When these signs become all too frequent, you must determine if they are just the consequence of an especially stressful period or if it has become a pattern. When the warning signs become evident, it is time for you to seek help, either for yourself, or the person you are concerned about. The sooner you are able to address these symptoms, the sooner you will be able to find a solution. The most important thing to keep in mind is that these conditions are treatable, and you can go back to being your old self.

Chapter 2:

Gauging Your Stress Levels

GAUGING YOUR STRESS levels is a good way to find the source of your worry. It can also help you determine where you are in the spectrum of anxiety and depression. If your stress levels are extremely high, chances are you are worrying more, and your anxiety is also going to be high. When you find yourself extremely stressed, sometimes it can be helpful to gain outside help such as a therapist.

There are several ways that you can gauge your stress levels. The most common things that show signs of stress are your sleep habits, your social interactions, your overall mood, your eating habits, and how you handle stressful situations. Use these guidelines to figure out where you are on the stress scale.

Sleep Habits

HOW HAVE YOU BEEN SLEEPING? Do you get at least seven hours of sleep each night? How long do you lay in bed before falling asleep? When you have insomnia and can't sleep for long periods, or you lay in bed for long periods before falling asleep, this is a sign that you are extremely stressed.

Do you feel tired when you wake up after a full night of sleep? Do you wake up multiple times throughout the night? Do you have strange dreams or active dreams that make you wake up feeling exhausted? If the answer to any of these questions is yes, it means that you have a moderate stress level. Are you sleeping too much and still feeling tired? This can be a sign of depression, which is usually the result of high-stress levels. Sleeping too much can be a sure sign of trouble and a wake-up call to improve your mental health.

Social Interactions

YOUR RELATIONSHIPS and how you interact with others, as well as your social life, can be very telling about your stress levels. When we become stressed, we tend to cut ourselves off from others. We have trouble articulating our feelings and tend to lash out. How are your relationships faring as of late? Are you finding yourself feeling cut off from your spouse or family?

Are you going off on your own rather than spending time with your friends and family? If you were once close to people and used to spend a lot of time with them and that has changed, it is a sign of high stress. How do you interact with others? Do you lose patience with people easily? Are you snapping at people rather than answering questions and concerns? Do you voice your feelings or keep them hidden? A sure sign of extreme stress is that you are unable to pleasantly and patiently converse with others. If you find yourself snapping at everyone and losing your temper easily, it is likely that you are extremely stressed.

Do you find yourself canceling social engagements? When you do go to social engagements, do you find yourself drinking more than usual? Are you frequently off by yourself rather than interacting with the group? Do you find that you don't enjoy yourself during social engagements? If all of these questions were answered with a yes, you are extremely stressed. A few yes answers, or feeling this way only some of the time, points to mild stress.

Eating Habits

HOW IS YOUR APPETITE? Do you skip meals more frequently than usual? Do you forget to eat, or just not feel hungry at dinner time? A loss of appetite and resulting rapid weight loss is a sign that you are extremely stressed.

Do you find yourself binge eating after a day or two of barely eating at all? This can be a sign that you are moderately stressed. Your stress level is preventing you from wanting to eat at normal times, but your body is still maintaining its appetite. The result is binge eating, which can lead to weight gain. Have you noticed an increase in your weight even though your appetite has not changed? This can be a sign of high-stress levels. When you are stressed your body releases the hormone cortisol, which slows the metabolism and can lead to weight gain. If your eating habits haven't changed, but your weight has, this could be a sign that you are moderately stressed.

Overall Mood

HOW HAVE YOU BEEN FEELING lately? Have you been feeling not quite yourself? Do you lack enjoyment in activities that you typically enjoy? Perhaps you like to read but haven't been able to pick up and concentrate on a book. Perhaps you like to play with your children throughout the day, but find yourself unable to enjoy it as of late.

Are you feeling happy? Do you spend most of your time feeling sad or indifferent? Feelings of indifference are a sign of moderate stress levels, while feelings of being sad can be a sign of severe stress and oncoming depression.

Do you constantly feel on edge? Do you feel as though you are a ticking time bomb? This feeling is usually brought on by a decrease in serotonin production with an increase in epinephrine. It is your mind's way of saying it's time for fight or flight. When this happens, you are at risk for clinical anxiety or depression.

Smoking, Drinking and Other Habits

ARE YOU A SMOKER? YOUR smoking habits can tell a lot about your stress levels. If you have increased your smoking by a half or one pack a day or more, this is a definite sign that you are extremely stressed. Smokers tend to reach for a cigarette every time they are able and feel stressed. If you are smoking over two packs a day where you used to smoke only one, it's time to take action to reduce your stress levels.

The same can be said of those who drink. Have you gone from a single glass of wine in the evening to drinking an entire bottle? Have you gone from rarely drinking at all to drinking every night? If you find yourself drinking a lot more than you used to, it could be a sign that you are falling into a pattern of high stress or depression.

Really, an increase in any vice or bad habit that is used to combat stress is a clear sign that you are in trouble. High stress can lead to gambling addictions, drug addictions, and alcoholism. It is important to recognize these signs for what they are so that you can combat the cause of the problem and save your health.

Using Journaling to Gauge Stress Levels

SOMETIMES WHEN LIFE is hectic, it can be hard to remember the little things. You may not remember how you've slept beyond the last couple of nights. You may not remember what you did or did not eat last week. Gauging your stress level requires looking at your habits over a period of time, usually at least two weeks. Journaling can be a great tool for gauging your stress levels. Get a plain notebook and assign a page for each day. Keep track of your overall mood, what you ate, how you slept and how much you slept, and any events that happened that day that could account for your mood or stress level. Keep this journal for two weeks. At the end of the two weeks, go back through the entries with the questions from above in mind. You may want to keep a separate entry just for your findings and to summarize the information from the two weeks of journaling.

If you are stressed, you will begin to notice patterns as you work your way back through the entries. Journaling is a great habit to form and continue as you work through trying to lower your stress and stop worrying. It can help you see how you have made progress as you work through your worry and anxiety, which can help give your overall mood a boost. When you have journaled for two weeks, and your stress levels are clearly low, you will be able to look back at the previous entries and take pride in your success.

Chapter 3

The Warning Signs Depression

When most folks think about anxiety and depression, they tend to think about a full-down, massive breakdown in which the sufferer is unable to function as a regular human being. These are often depicted in Hollywood films and television programs as people who cannot even get out of bed and take control of their own lives.

While this type of reaction can happen, especially when depression sets in at its most extreme levels, the fact of the matter is that most people go through their day-to-day lives functioning at a seemingly normal level. In the previous chapter, I mentioned how high-functioning depression is a condition with which many successful people commonly live.

They are able to function through their daily lives and routines, and apparently, not give off any signs that they are suffering from any kind of depression whatsoever. Even in those cases, where successful people seem to have everything under control, there are warning signs that give away a person's internal emotional condition.

Let's start off with anxiety. Anxiety is a debilitating condition which can hinder people from enjoying normal interaction with their surroundings. Consider social anxiety. When a person suffers from social anxiety, they may have trouble adapting and adjusting to the people around them. These sufferers may have troubling fitting into social groups like sports teams, classrooms, social clubs, churches, or any other place where groups of people gather.

Of course, there is a difference between a naturally shy person and a person who may be diagnosed with Social Anxiety Disorder. For naturally shy people, interacting with others on a regular basis may prove to be a challenging situation. For those who actually suffer from Social Anxiety Disorder, there is a deeper cause to their affliction.

These causes may range from traumatic childhood events to physical issues in the brain. Nevertheless, anxiety, in all its forms, can keep a person from enjoying a healthy and productive life. One of the most common factors which affect anxiety is stress.

Stress is a powerful force which can weaken a person's natural mental defenses to a point where they become excessively worried, or concerned, about what may happen to them. Sure, there are logical reasons why a person may become overly anxious. For instance, if you are going through a difficult financial situation in which you have lost your job, need to pay the bills and are at risk of losing your home, the anxiety will definitely get a grip on you.

In this case, it is natural that a person has trouble sleeping, become irritable, lose appetite, or binge eat and gain weight, increase alcohol and drug consumption, engage is risk practices such a reckless driving, or even become isolated and reduce social interaction. All of these symptoms, while concerning, point to a struggle with anxiety. Given the circumstances in which the stressful condition was created, all of these symptoms may go away when the individual's financial situation is solved. Then, they can get their life back on track through rest and possibly medication and therapy. The symptoms which we have outlined begin in such a subtle manner that they are often imperceptible and go unnoticed. Many times, these symptoms are dismissed as, "being stressed out," or "going through a rough patch." But what ends up happening is that these feelings fester, and over time, can lead to debilitating anxiety, or depression. In the previous chapter, we defined depression as having extreme feelings of dejection and despondency. This could not be more accurate.

Depression is a feeling in which the sufferer feels like all hope is lost. This is where suicidal thoughts find fertile soil. If untreated, depression may lead to somatization in which any number of physical ailments may develop. These physical ailments can range from migraine headaches to diabetes, heart disease and even autoimmune diseases such as lupus. As you can see, depression is serious business.

Often, depression is seen as a psychological and mental disorder which requires medication as the first course of treatment. While there is no doubt that antidepressants such as Prozac, Zoloft or Paxil, which essentially inhibit certain chemical reactions in the brain, can be suitable options to help folks get back on their feet, the fact of the matter is that medication only treats the superficial ailments caused by depression.

In order to get to the root cause of depression, therapy is often required. With therapy, individuals can drill down and see what is fueling their feelings of dejection and despair. Many times, chronic stress, which can lead to burnout, also leads to depression. When an individual is exposed to tremendous amounts of stress over prolonged periods of time, they can fall into a depressive condition in which their entire personality seems to morph completely. Think of soldiers who go off to war.

A regular, healthy human being that is exposed to the large amounts of stress, such as war, may experience Post-Traumatic Stress Disease (PTSD). PTSD is a condition which arises from a singular, traumatic event that leaves an individual debilitated and unable to cope with everyday life. This condition is treatable, and recovery usually begins by removing the individual from the traumatic experience.

Now, imagine a soldier that has done several tours of duty in a war zone. This individual may be subjected to so much stress, that their entire personality morphs into someone else. They may go from being a kind, well-adjusted individual, to becoming violent and aggressive with the least amount of provocation. This change may be perfectly obvious to those who have not seen this person for a while. But for the individuals themselves, spotting these behavioral changes is virtually impossible.

That is how a person can descend into depression without even noticing it. So, what can you do to spot depression in time? You can be on the lookout for unusual behavioral changes such as emotional outbursts, unprovoked crying, or unusual euphoria. Yes, even euphoria and "joy" can become warning signs. This type of behavior is evident in unruly children. When a child enters a depressive stage, they will often act out in violent and mischievous ways.

The reason for this lies in the fact that the individual is experiencing violent mood swings. And so, getting a grip on their emotions can become a hard task. That is why you must keep an eye on your loved ones especially when they are going through a hard time emotionally. You must learn to interpret outburst and even destructive behavior as a cry for attention. This can be seen in excessive alcohol and drug consumption, reckless behavior such as driving and firearm use, or disengaging attitudes such as withdrawal and isolation.

If you are reading this and feel that some of these symptoms may apply to you, seek help at once. Find someone in whom you can confide. Ask them to take you to a proper healthcare professional who can provide you with alternatives on how to deal with your feelings. Please bear in mind that asking for help is not a sign of weakness. In fact, it takes a great deal of strength to admit you need help. So, don't delay. Your family and loved ones will admire your courage. And, they will surely help you overcome what you are going through.

Chapter 4:

What causes anxiety and depression?

In previous chapters, we have already touched upon the cause of anxiety and depression. We have discussed the triggers that most commonly induce anxiety and depression in individuals. In this chapter, we will take a much closer look at the causes which can lead to anxiety and depression and how you can begin to understand why this is happening to you, or someone you know.

The most important benefit of understanding the causes of anxiety and depression is that you will see that it is not the sufferer's fault, but rather, this person is a victim of circumstance. So, let's get started with the causes of anxiety.

Causes of anxiety
Generally speaking, anxiety is mainly a psychological and emotional condition. While we have established that

this condition can have physical effects on the sufferer, it mostly triggers a psychological and emotional response which can, in the most extreme cases, render a person unable to function normally in their regular, day-to-day lives.

Now, all of us experience anxiety to a greater, or lesser, extent. Allow me to elaborate. Imagine you are a student and you are prepping for your final exams. There is a lot on the line, be it a passing grade, or a high grade which will allow you to get into the program of your choice at the school you most desire to enter.

So, you decide to put the pedal to the metal and buckle down on your schoolwork. Since you have a lot riding on your finals, the stress of getting good grades begins to get to you. You begin to have trouble sleeping, you may be losing your appetite, or binging on junk food, some individuals decide to take up smoking or drinking excessive amounts of coffee, or in some cases, show signs of irritability and overall bad mood.

Now, while this may seem like a "normal" reaction to high levels of stress, the person would go back to their normal behavioral patterns once finals are over and the stressful situation has been removed from the life of this individual. After a period of rest and recovery, the person goes back to their usual way of life having learned a valuable life lesson.

This type of reaction to anxiety caused by a significantly stressful situation is quite common and should not be a cause for alarm. But what if this anxious behavioral pattern becomes all too common? This is why it is important to differentiate one type of anxiety from another. Anxiety due to a heavy course load is one thing, but it's another completely different thing to shut yourself off from the world because you cannot establish relationships with other types. As such, the five most common types of anxiety are as follows:

1. General Anxiety Disorder
2. Obsessive-Compulsive Disorder
3. Panic Disorder
4. Post-Traumatic Stress Disorder
5. Social Anxiety Disorder

As you can see, we have already discussed these disorders to some extent. With the exception of PTSD, we have indicated how these types of anxiety all have their roots in some type of childhood trauma. Often, this trauma stems from some type of prolonged abusive or traumatic situation.

Think of situations in which children come from abusive homes, or backgrounds, in which they face neglect, physical harm, psychological and emotion distress, and even sexual abuse. While the most extreme cases of childhood trauma can lead to more serious conditions such as Dissociative Personality Disorder, prolonged exposure to trauma and stress can lead to the development of more generalized anxiety.

Of course, the development of anxiety does not necessarily have its roots in childhood. In fact, people who come from loving homes may develop some type anxiety disorder. But how? Well, in the case of PTSD, anxiety can stem from one, singular incident such as a car accident, the violent death of a loved one, or an incredibly stressful situation such as financial distress.

Anxiety can build up over time to a degree where the individual who suffers from prolonged exposure to stressful situations may not be able to fully recover once they have been extricated from the stressful environment which caused these feelings.

Think of people in high-stress profession such as stock trading. The average lifespan of a Wall Street stock trader is about 10 years. Why? Well, it's an incredibly stressful profession which demands constant attention.

Most stock traders are plugged in for long hours with very few breaks in between. Since financial markets essentially run on 24 hours a day, stock traders may feel compelled to keep their foot on the gas even when they are officially off work. In addition, the added burden that comes with the responsibility of managing large sums of money is hard enough.

Most stock traders also face pressure from investors to make the best possible returns on the money invested. This leads them to make risky decisions which may or may not pay off in the end. The stress that comes from the uncertainty of a stock deal can keep a fella up for nights. This is why alcohol and drug abuse has been seen among stock traders. These substances are used as coping mechanisms which end up costing individuals a lot more than then produce.

Often, individuals who resort to substance abuse as a coping mechanism end up with a greater problem which is having to deal with addiction issues on top of their anxiety. When this occurs, medication may be the only way to help an anxiety sufferer get back on track since the body, unfortunately, becomes used to those unusually high levels of stress. In the end, the best course of action for people who find themselves in high-stress professions is to seek healthy coping mechanisms, such as mindfulness, which can ultimately help them deal with their anxiety in a much more productive manner thereby leading to a more well-adjusted mental condition.

Causes of depression

However, some folks end up being exposed to large amounts of stress for prolonged periods of time such as years on end. These folks may end up developing what is known as "chronic stress." Chronic stress, given that it is a "chronic" condition may never fully dissipate. As such, chronic stress is not the type of condition which will go away after a week on the beach. As a matter of fact, chronic stress often leads to burnout, a condition which is often a precursor to full-blown depression.

When burnout sets in, the sufferer finds themselves feeling constantly fatigued, sleep deprived, usually overeating, abusing substances such as alcohol, caffeine or drugs, and even resorting prescription medication abuse.

Burnout tends to be confused with depression and depression tends to be confused with burnout. There are times when doctors prescribe some antidepressants and a good vacation thinking that sufferers are just tired and need a break.

This is a critical mistake since a depressed individual actually requires a lot more than just a break. Therefore, understanding that the root cause of a person's depression may be related to burnout and chronic stress is the first step toward helping the sufferer get back on track. Other times, depression as deep and profound emotional root. This could be the result of a traumatic experience such as the death of a loved one.

This is especially true when a person dies unexpectedly or passes on after a long bout with a terrible illness. The family members who are left behind are often burned out, emotionally distressed and in a deep state of sadness.

While it is perfectly normal to grieve over the death of a loved one, a profound sadness, which goes untreated, may end up becoming a full-blown depression. Once a full-blown depression sets in, the afflicted individual may become too affected to carry on with a normal life. In addition, depression may take years to develop. As we have pointed out, chronic stress can be an underlying factor for depression.

This is due to the fact that stress goes untreated, festers and then develops into a much deeper condition. Often times, depression has a root in childhood. We have already indicated how abusive homes may lead individuals to develop some type of anxiety disorder. But it is also common to see adults who have come from abusive childhoods to end up developing some type of depression.

This type of depression can be categorized as "major depression" and can range from a debilitating condition in which the individual may need a combination of medication and therapy in order to cope with the situation or may need stronger treatment options such as rehab when there is drug or prescription medication abuse.

Then, there are other types of depression which may stem from purely physiological conditions such as Bipolar Disorder or Post-partum Depression. In both cases, the root causes are physiological and have more to the with the proper functioning of the brain than any psychological or emotional causes. In the case of Bipolar Disorder, medication is almost always the only choice sufferers have. This enables them to rebalance the chemical composition in their brains and regain a great deal of normalcy in their daily functioning.

In the case of Post-partum Depression, the chemical and hormonal imbalances leftover from pregnancy may end up causing the most common symptoms such as sadness, fatigue, irritability and just a plain sense of melancholy. This is a condition which can be treated by a combination of both therapy and medication.

Depression is almost always a condition that never fully dissipates, even over time and with the right treatment. Unlike anxiety, which tends to show signs of recovery once the person has received treatment, depression can linger for years on end, and with frequent flare-ups. For anyone who has gone through depression or has cared for someone who has dealt with the depression, will understand that there are "good days and bad days." During "good days," the sufferer is often happy and in a good mood.

During "bad days" the flare-ups may range from just regular moodiness to an allout collapse. This is when you might see some folks going through periods of uncontrollable crying and sadness, to their body simply shutting off while they sleep for several hours on end.

This volatility in depressed people's moods is generally induced by certain "triggers." For instance, a depressed individual who is grieving over the loss of a loved one may experience a trigger when they come into contact with certain memories, places or objects.

Therefore, it is vital to learn to recognize these triggers and avoid them as much as possible. When depression is a purely, physiological condition, the sufferer needs to follow their doctor's instructions carefully, take their medication (if prescribed) and maintain a generally healthy and balanced lifestyle.

This last point is very important since the onset of a flare-up can happen at any time. Thus, it is important for the individual to recognize their triggers and act accordingly when symptoms are imminent. In such cases, when the sufferer is well aware of the triggers which active flare-ups, it's important for them to be able to count on family and friends who can support them while they deal with the onset of negative feelings.

This is especially true when the sufferer is exhibiting suicidal thoughts and tendencies. In those cases, these individuals need constant monitoring. Otherwise, they may end up setting of a trigger which may lead to them acting upon such harmful thoughts. This is why I advocate the families and friends of depressed individuals to build communication and trust so that they are able to support and assist the depressed individual whenever they need to. Unfortunately, those who suffer in silence lack this type of support. And many times, friends and family learn about the truth until after it's too late. That is why it is of the utmost importance that depressed individuals seek help as soon as possible. It may very well save their lives.

Chapter 5:

What's Next After Diagnosis?

At this point, we have discussed causes of anxiety and depression, as well as, the symptoms which can be evidenced in people with either one of these conditions. We have also stressed the importance of seeking help upon the realization that you, or someone you know, might have this condition.

This is the hardest part: admitting that you need help and then looking for it. If you are trying to reach someone who is being afflicted by this condition, it can seem virtually impossible to get through to them. Sufferers may even say they want help, but when it actually comes down to going in for diagnosis and treatment, you may encounter resistance.

In such cases, short of literally dragging someone to the doctor's office, there isn't much you can do to *force* someone to seek help. I used the term "force" since you really can't force anyone to seek help. This is something that each individual must really want. Of course, there are cases when you must act in this manner. For instance, you might in the case of someone who is a danger to themselves.

In which case, you need to step in right away before they hurt themselves. Short of such a case, the ideal scenario would be to have the afflicted individual become aware that they need help and that there are healthcare professionals out there who are qualified in providing them with the help and support they need in order to get better. So, the first step begins with admitting that you need help. When you are able to admit that you need help, you can then go out and seek it.

Generally speaking, you can go to your primary care physician who would be ready to provide you with immediate treatment. This could be in the form of medication which can help treat the most immediate symptoms such as insomnia, or mild antidepressants. At that point, your primary care physician would most likely refer you to a psychiatrist who can then begin a series of tests in order to determine if you, or the person you are caring for, indeed has a condition like depression or anxiety.

If you happen to find yourself having serious suicidal thoughts, or if the person you are caring for is showing serious signs of harming themselves, you may choose to take them into the emergency room. In this case, the most immediate course of treatment would be medication. This medication would most likely be a course in antidepressants or even a solid dose of sleeping pills.

Now, whether you visit the doctor on your own accord, or through an emergency room visit, a psychiatrist would most likely become involved in providing you with an official diagnosis. Other times, you may be referred to a neurologist to determine if there might be a physiological condition afflicting the individual. That evaluation may lead to a course of medication designed specifically for the condition affecting the individual. If the cause is determined to be psychological and/or emotional, medication would be followed up with therapy and counseling. In this case, therapy and counseling are intended to help the individual understand why they feel the way they do and find positive ways of coping with depression or anxiety. Now, an official depression or anxiety diagnosis is by no means a stigma.

Unfortunately, there is a high degree of ignorance surrounding mental health issues. In mainstream society, people who suffer from depression or anxiety are seen as weak and unable to cope with life. This is why many choose to suffer in silence and try to deal with things on their own.

Granted, some individuals show a tremendous amount of fortitude and manage to pull through on their own. But there is also an equal number of individuals who do not manage to pull through and end up harming themselves. Sadly, some of these cases end up in tragedy such as suicide. A positive depression or anxiety diagnosis is not a life sentence either. Sure, the severity of the condition may leave a person dependent on medication for the rest of their lives. This is something that must not be ruled out.

Conversely, it must not be ruled out that with medication and therapy, as well as, other treatment options, an individual can regain a sense of normalcy in their lives and become free of their dependency on medication.

While becoming free from medication is the ideal scenario, it must be understood that reliance on medication may be the only effective treatment option. This is especially true in cases where individuals exhibit conditions such as Bipolar Disorder or severe cases of PTSD.

Perhaps the biggest factor in helping a person through depression and anxiety, especially in severe cases, is creating a loving and stable environment around them in which the sufferer feels safe and appreciated. This is especially true with children and teenagers. When children and teenagers find themselves diagnosed with a condition such as depression or anxiety, their fears and insecurities come to the forefront. This will lead them to exhibit aggressive and erratic behavior which may stunt their development at a certain stage.

This is why a loving environment would enable them to feel secure and allow them to process their feelings. In the case of adults, having a loving and supportive environment is equally important. By surrounding the sufferer with a caring environment, they will begin to feel secure and may be willing to open up about how they feel. This is crucial when you consider how hard it can be for someone to show their vulnerability.

That is why a loving and supportive environment, in addition to medication and therapy, and other wellness techniques such as mindfulness, will become vital to helping you, or the person you care about, overcome this condition. So, I would encourage you to build a support network around yourself so

that you can get the emotional support that you need in order to ensure you get the help you need, or that you are there to provide the love and support your loved ones need.

Chapter 6:

The Worry Trick to Beat Anxiety and Depression

In previous chapters, we have discussed traditional treatment options for anxiety and depression.

Traditional treatment options generally revolve around a combination of medication and therapy. This approach generally presents good results.

In fact, the combination of medication and therapy tends to be the best course of action, especially in cases when there is Major Depression, Bipolar Disorder, or even Social Anxiety Disorder. In these cases, medication is almost always the most effective treatment option as the symptoms are so severe that individuals may find themselves unable to function properly.

Furthermore, those cases in which individuals cannot take care of themselves, or even show signs of potentially hurting themselves, medication followed by therapy, usually in the form of one-on-one sessions or group counseling usually provides the best results. But what about those cases in which symptoms are not as severe? What about those cases in which folks are simply stressed out or a just blue?

When this happens, it is important to consider how you can address these issues without resorting to medication. I always stress the fact that medication is not the only treatment option available. While medication may be the easiest course of treatment, it can also generate dependency in those folks who take it. Of course, dependency is not an ideal scenario as this may level to prescription drug abuse among other potential secondary effects of prolonged medication.

As we have also stated earlier, it is crucial to address the root causes of anxiety and depression. Often these conditions have psychological and emotional causes. When you are able to identify them, you can begin to address them in a holistic manner. Other times, counseling may be the best way for you to address those root causes.

You might find yourself in a support group in which similar folks can share their experiences in order to help you come to grips with what you are feeling. In those cases, therapy and counseling provide tremendous benefits, particularly when considering that anxiety and depression in their initial stages are perfectly treatable and can lead the individual to make a full recovery without any lasting effects.

As I have stated earlier, untreated symptoms can fester until they become full-blown anxiety and depression. This may lead to individuals to become debilitated and unable to cope with the reality they are facing. When this happens, helping individuals recover and regain a sense of normalcy may prove to become incredibly difficult.

Consequently, catching these conditions as they begin becomes an imperative measure to be taken. So, please go back, if you must, to the chapter in which we discussed the early warning signs that you can look out for in yourself, or in someone you suspect may be going through this. As such, we will be looking at an additional way to help overcome anxiety and depression that are not related to medication and therapy. These are ways in which you can find peace, solace, and comfort, especially when you are down in the dumps. In addition, these strategies can help you deal with your anxiety and depression proactively especially if you are already on medication and going to therapy.

Mindfulness and meditation

Mindfulness is the first step in helping anxiety and depression sufferers cope with their symptoms. This practice involves meditation and relaxation techniques which can help you deal with the symptoms associated with anxiety and depression.

In particular, these techniques can help when you feel the onset of symptoms that may lead to an anxiety attack or simply get your down. The practice of mindfulness techniques will help you get a grip on your feelings by helping you develop a sense of introspection, that is, understand why you feel the way you do and recognize when symptoms, such as negative thoughts, are starting to get a hold of you. So, you can begin with good, old-fashioned meditation.

Now, meditation isn't about sitting in a quiet garden, breathing, and repeating some mantra. Meditation is about listening to yourself, your thoughts and being able to examine your feelings from a third-party perspective. When you are able to achieve this, you will be able to figure out what triggers your feelings. For instance, it could be a repressed childhood memory, an object that reminds you of someone or visiting a place that sets off the recollection of an unpleasant experience.

As such, meditation, as a regular practice, will help you gain more control over your feelings and how you perceive yourself. Here is a simple practice that I like to do especially when I am stressed out. I like to find a quiet moment in my home and sit in my favorite chair. I know this can be extremely difficult to do especially if you have children running around the house all day. In fact, believe it or not, I have done this in my car when I cannot get peace anywhere else.

To start off, sit in your favorite chair and close your eyes. Place your hands on your lap and begin to breathe slowly. If you find that you are heaving, try to slow your breathing down by taking deep breaths. You can inhale, hold for three seconds and then exhale until you feel your lungs are empty. Then inhale again and hold. While doing this, try to "listen" to yourself breathing. As you listen to your breathing, you will be bombarded by all kinds of thoughts. These thoughts may range from random stuff you have seen throughout the course of your day, to the insane and unpleasant thoughts that might be haunting you.

Try your best to not dwell on the bills, work, your boss, kids, car trouble, the loved ones that are gone and even the traumatic experiences you have gone through. They will come at you from all angles. But just let them pass. Watch them fly by. One after another. Imagine that you are just an observer watching a show. Concentrate on your breathing. If you feel the anxiety building up, then pay attention to why you are feeling that way. Why are you feeling the way you do? What thoughts are triggering this reaction? When you pay close attention to those feelings, you become more aware of your triggers. Perhaps it was something someone said to you that hurt you deeply. Perhaps it was something you saw which reminded you of an unpleasant, or even, traumatic experience. Whatever the case, focus on why you are feeling the way you do. But don't stop breathing!

As the anxiety builds up, you may find yourself beginning to quicken your breath. That is where you need to slow things down. Slow your breathing down and focus on "listening" to each breath. As you do this, you will find yourself managing to get a hold of your thoughts and feelings.

Don't be afraid to face your thought. After all, they are just thoughts. As scary and daunting as they may be, they are just thoughts. They are in your head. So, you have nothing to be afraid of. This practice is great especially for folks who have trouble sleeping. In fact, some folks like to listen to soft music while doing they are engaged in this exercise. Personally, I love soft piano music.

This type of music is soothing, and it helps me concentrate better on my breathing. As a matter of fact, this exercise works so well that I have fallen asleep quite often. As I said, it is great when you can't sleep because all sorts of thoughts are racing through your mind. I would encourage you to try this exercise when you are tired, and you can't sleep. You can lie in your bed, in a comfortable position and picture your thoughts, one by one, as they fly by the eyes of your mind. Soon, you will find yourself out like a light.

Being present
But mindfulness isn't just about meditation. Mindfulness is a 24/7 activity which you do anywhere, anytime. A great mindfulness exercise is to be "present." When you are present, you are not worrying about the past of the future. You are only concerned about the "here," and the "now." Sure, we can't erase the past with a giant magic marker, and we can't dismiss the future as we need to prepare as best we can. But being present means that, at this moment, there is nothing else around you.

You are the only thing that exists. This will help you focus on what's going on at present and nothing else. Being present is not about "forgetting" about the past and the future, it's about not concerning yourself with them. The past is done, and it's behind you while the future may not even happen; hence the trick! You might be worried about something that may not even happen! That is how being present is exactly the best way you can let go of the future. Let go of the future?

Exactly! When you stop focusing on what may or may not happen and prepare for anything that may come, you will put yourself in a great position to come out on top. Consider this example: Let's say that you are anxious about your health. You might be feeling very concerned about paying for your healthcare costs. So, you could decide to purchase some insurance for yourself and your family. In this way, you are covered in case anything happens. By having a proactive approach (getting insurance), you are covering your position in such a way that you won't have to worry about how you will pay for your bills since you already have coverage. Now, this example may seem very simplistic, but it goes to show how something simple can set you up for something larger down the road. The same goes for the past. When you dwell on the past, you are dwelling on something you cannot change. What does that mean?

Well, it means that there is no use in dwelling on something you have no control over. The past is done. So, there is nothing more to be. You are now in control of the present. This is why it is vitally important to live in the present; in the "here" and the "now." As you gain more practice and experience with controlling your current situation and surroundings, you will be able to make the most of the situations that are at hand. You will be able to relinquish control over things which you may not have any control over.

The case for a healthy diet and exercise

One commonly overlooked alternative is a healthy diet and regular exercise. This combination will help you feel much better about yourself. As you become healthier and fitter, you will get a boost to your self-esteem. As your selfesteem climbs, you will be able to focus more on continuing to improve yourself. Furthermore, it is highly recommended that you moderate your intake of certain foods and drinks which may be harming you.

For example, consumption of excessive amounts of caffeine, energy drinks and other stimulating substances can cause you to have momentary bursts of energy and euphoria but may leave you down in the dumps when the effects of the stimulants wear off. In other cases, excessive consumption of junk food may lead you to binge eating. This is especially true when food is used as a coping mechanism.

When this happens, you may find yourself consuming large amounts of food which is high in fat, cholesterol, sodium, and sugars. This can lead you to become obese and even trigger other health issues such as diabetes and heart disease, among other conditions. In addition, it is also recommended that sufferers of depression and anxiety "clean up their act," that is, reduce, if not completely cut out, cigarettes, marijuana, or any other "recreational" use of drugs. Also, reducing, if not eliminating, alcohol consumption is ideal during the recovery process. Just like you may become dependent on medication during your recovery, you may also become dependent on other substances.

This is where it is important for you to take into account the need to get away from excessive consumption of certain substances. As for exercise, exercising regularly is a great way to boost your mood. When you engage in any type of physical activity, your brain begins to release endorphins. This is the hormone that is associated with good feelings. That is why you tend to get a good vibe after you have finished your workout. Also, trying your best to be fit will make you feel better about yourself.

Consequently, when you feel good about yourself, you will be able to get a better handle on negative thoughts. As you become fitter and get into better shape, this will boost your mood, and your confidence, since you will be working on a better version of yourself. After all, who doesn't want to look fit and attractive? Exercise should also be about engaging in activities which you enjoy. For instance, there is a sport that you enjoy playing such as basketball or soccer. So, when you take part in this sport, your mood will begin to improve since you are doing something you like.

I recall a friend that once told me about why he took up tennis. He was a high-power sales executive. He was constantly on the phone making deals and hardly had any type of slow down. He had a tough boss that demanded results. My friend was clearly one of the best at what he did, but after a while, he began to feel the effects of constant stress due to a high-paced life.

So, he took up tennis. But tennis wasn't the first sport he had tried out. In fact, he had tried a number of sports and gave up on all of them. Why? Well, he told me how he was unable to concentrate on what he was doing. Thoughts about work and meeting targets would always come rushing to his mind.

Consequently, he couldn't enjoy what he was doing as he was constantly worrying about the work he had left behind. Then, he discovered tennis. In his own words, he told me how hard it was for him to hit the ball. So, he really needed to focus and concentrate in order for him to hit the ball. Voila! That did it. He was able to find a sport in which he could concentrate fully and forget about the office. Perhaps his need to focus on concentrate on the ball was due to a lack and hand-eye coordination. But whatever it was, tennis became an outlet for him.

Soon, he made buddies at his tennis club. This enabled him to get a grip on his anxiety and improve his overall health and wellbeing.

Therefore, I would encourage you to find a sport, or exercise routine, which can help you keep your mind off the stressors which are bearing down upon your mental health.

Aromatherapy
One very discreet way of keeping your negative thoughts in check can be through aromatherapy. By surrounding yourself with pleasant scents, you are sending a positive signal to your brain. These pleasant scents will help you keep a positive vibe through your usual environment. In particular, scents such as lavender and vanilla are great for helping folks relax. Nevertheless, I would encourage you to find your favorite scent and sprinkle around your surroundings.

This could be in your office, your bedroom, and certainly in your car. Also, burning incense is a great way of achieving that soothing effect that comes with pleasant scents. While you may not be able to burn incense everywhere you go, you can certainly keep some sticks handy at home and your office.

It has been shown that pleasant smells, even from perfume and cologne, can help reduce anxiety significantly. So, don't be skimpy on the pleasant scents. Get that perfume, or cologne, that you love. Ask your significant other to wear that scent you love. And don't forget to use essential oils to give your surroundings that extra soothing touch.

Don't forget about the visuals
It is amazing how visuals have a positive, and negative, impact on a person's mood. A cluttered and messy environment is often conducive to feeling even worse than you already do. In contrast, a neat and tidy situation will help you feel much better about yourself. This is why it is highly recommended to keep a nice and tidy environment around you. This applies to both home and work.

And, it also goes for cars and even wallets. When you find yourself in a cluttered environment which may even be full of useless things, you will make it hard for yourself to find a safe place to call home. You may end up becoming anxious and stressed out because you can't find what you are looking for. In addition, a messy situation is almost always a precursor to depression.

So, take it upon yourself to keep your car, bedroom, office and living room as neat as you can. Now, I am not saying that you need to become obsessive about cleanliness. What I am saying is that a neat and tidy environment will do wonders to helping you feel much better about yourself.

So, it certainly pays for you to take the extra time to make sure that you have everything you need handy. By having everything in one spot, and knowing where everything is, you will be able to reduce anxiety by providing yourself with certainty and security.

Get a pet
Pets have been found to help reduce anxiety and depression. In particular, it has been found that dogs can help anxious folks find a faithful companion who will help them find a balance. Something as simple as petting a dog can help reduce anxiety drastically. I have known folks who get a dog or cat, and just by playing with them, caressing them, and just having a pal around all the time, helps reduce anxiety by a significant margin. Having pets can also help depressed folks get better by providing companionship especially when depressed folks suffer in silence.

In essence, what a pet does is that it provides unconditional companionship especially when the sufferer feels they are misunderstood or unjustly signaled out for whatever reason. Since pets cannot speak and behave much the same way humans do, sufferers find a companion who is not judgmental.

Often pets, are there to provide solace during times of hardship. While dogs and cats are the most common choices, other folks enjoy pet birds, fish, and even hamsters. The fact of the matter is that having a pet helps deflect negative energy into something more positive, such as taking care of a pet.

By being there for your pet, you too can get a sense of purpose. Other times, pets can become that impartial and attentive listener who is not going to pass judgment on the way you feel. They will kindly listen and give you all the love they are capable of giving. One effective treatment option for anxiety, especially in children, is equineassisted therapy. This type of therapy has been shown to help children relax and become more confident. It has proven to be especially effective with

children who have a disability of some sort. Horse have such a powerful effect on humans that the bond a persona may make with a horse, especially for children, will inspire confidence and security.

This is what enables equine-assisted therapy to truly become effective. So, I would encourage you to look into this, especially if you have a child or teen who may be coping with anxiety or depression.

Seeking a higher power
There are times when seeking a higher power can help depressed folks kick the blues. By engaging in spiritual activities, anxious or depressed individuals may find comfort and solace in a place of worship.

Generally speaking, seeking to connect with your spiritual self will allow you to connect with a deeper purpose for your life. After all, we all have a purpose in life. The challenge is trying to find out what it is. This is where anxious and depressed individuals find a purpose in life. This enables them to kick the blues and channel their energy into seeking a deeper connection with the overall mission in life.

Seeking a higher power is especially forceful for depressed individuals. When a depressed person feels that there is a connection with a superior being, they feel that they are not alone. For those who have firm religious convictions, they can find comfort in knowing that their faith is capable of helping them get through whatever crisis they are going through. Other times, churches provide a social group which can serve as a support group. I have personally found that prayer groups in churches really do make amazing miracles. It is the power of this collective energy which makes the sufferer feel confident and reassured. This positive energy becomes a new mindset for depressed and anxious folks.

One other significant strategy is not highlight passages in your book of worship. These passages should offer you consolation when you are down and serve as a reminder that there is always some higher power with you which can help you get through whatever you are going through. As your spiritual connection deepens, you will be well on your way to recovery.

A Fresh start
In addition to everything we have highlighted in this chapter, a fresh start can prove to be just what the doctor ordered. There are times when depression kicks due to a succession of adverse events. For example, you might lose your job, your house, your car, and even end up in divorce. Such a traumatic experience can certainly lead to serious anxiety and depression conditions. So, as a complement to any, and all, of the options we have described in this chapter, what you may need is a fresh start.

Often, this takes the form of moving to another city and starting over. This is typical when a specific geographical location makes it unbearable for the sufferer and sets off triggers continuously. I have found it useful to wipe the slate clean at regular intervals. For instance, I use each new month as a new opportunity to make something great of myself. This is especially true when you have a bad streak.

The start of a new month can provide you with a psychological milestone whereby you can start over and put those negative experiences behind you. The only time of year I would caution you to take care in starting over is

New Year's. This occasion is a classic time when people, in general, get down in the dumps. For a person dealing with depression and anxiety, it may become tempting you make some New Year's resolutions which may or may not work out. Nevertheless, a psychological signpost such as the start of a new year can provide you with the opportunity to push the "reset" button. Sure, it's not quite as easy as it sounds, but you can take the first step toward changing your situation and the way you feel about your surroundings.

Final thoughts
In this chapter, we discussed various ways in which you can address anxiety and depression from a completely different perspective that goes beyond therapy and medication. While this approach Is certainly effectively in helping most folks get their lives back on track, the implementation of any of the strategies discussed in this chapter will help sufferers get back on track and stay there.

So, if you are down in the dumps or someone you know is not feeling well, any of these tips will help boost their overall confidence and self-esteem. I am
certain that these tips and techniques will go a long way toward ensuring that you, or your loved ones, will continue to be healthy and productive members of society.

Chapter 7:

Understanding the Different Types of Depression

Thus far, we have discussed what depression is, its symptoms and treatment options. We have also touched upon the general definition of depression, that is, a profound state of dejection and despondency.

Yet, there are specific types of depression, or division, into which this condition can be classified into. So, in this chapter, we will be taking a closer look at each one of these divisions in order to gain a better understanding of the specific types of depression which can affect an individual and also learn about the difference between each type of depression.

Major depression
This first type of depression is known as "major depression." We have already discussed this type of depression at length. So, it's worth noting that a person may be diagnosed with this type of depression when they exhibit five or more of the symptoms associated with depression which are:
1.Chronic fatigue

2.Weight loss or gain

3.Trouble sleeping

4.Sleeping too much

5.Lack of focus

6.Loss of interest in pleasant activities

7.Withdrawal from social interaction

8.Suicidal thoughts

9.Feelings of guilt

10.Unusual irritability

These symptoms, while not exhaustive, are the hallmarks of major depression. As such, when a person consistently exhibits these symptoms, they may be diagnosed with major depression and provided with treatment options such as those already discussed in previous chapters.

Bipolar Disorder
Bipolar Disorder (BD), is considered to be a type of depression and is generally attributed to physiological causes. This condition is highlighted by violent mood swings which switch from opposite ends of the spectrum.

For example, a person with BD may be happily enjoying an activity and then suddenly become profoundly melancholy at the drop of a hat. Specific events generally trigger these type of mood swings. Since physiological factors typically cause this condition, medication is almost always prescribed along with therapy in order for the sufferer to become familiar with the options available to them in terms of getting a handle on this condition.

Season Affective Disorder
Season Affective Disorder (SAD), is a type of depression which is associated with seasonal changes in weather patterns. It is attributed to a lack of sunshine and weather conditions associated with spring and summer. SAD is common in countries where there are harsh winters or significant rainfall. Specifically, SAD is triggered by the persistence of weather conditions which limit a person's ability to enjoy common activities and limit their mobility. As such, they may become saddened by their inability to go out and enjoy their surroundings.
For this type of depression, a doctor may prescribe a mild antidepressant, though the use of techniques such as mindfulness and meditation is a great way of boosting mood and improving the sufferer's overall outlook in life.

Psychotic Depression
This type of depression contains, most, if not, all of the symptoms of major depression in addition to the following:
• Deep paranoia

• Hallucinations

• Delusions

These symptoms, in essence, transport the sufferer out of reality and into a state in which they feel, or believe, that something or someone is out to get them. A person exhibiting these symptoms may receive treatment for other mental disorders such as Schizophrenia, thought a healthcare professional would be advised to dig deeper into the causes of psychotic behavior.

One very important note is that psychotic episodes are not necessarily accompanied by outburst of violence in which the sufferer intends to hurt themselves or others around them. These episodes may be highlighted by uncontrollable crying or sobbing, crippling feelings which render the sufferer unable to take care of themselves and serious thoughts of suicide. Psychotic episodes are generally treated with sedatives in order to get the sufferer under control. In addition, strong antidepressant, or antipsychotic medication may be administered.

Post-Partum Depression

This type of depression follows childbirth. It can affect women of all shapes and sizes and cannot be attributed to any kind of physiological or emotional predisposition. Since it is generally hormonal, doctors may choose to prescribe a hormone regulatory course of treatment as opposed to antidepressants.

Women who are going to Post-partum Depression are encouraged to seek counseling as a means of understanding that they are going through and how they can manage their feelings. This condition generally dissipates over time and may not require further treatment. Care needs to be taken as untreated Post-partum Depression may fester and eventually develop into major depression.

Premenstrual Dysphoric Disorder (PMDD)

This type of depression can be evidenced prior to the beginning of a woman's period. Since it is hormonal, a doctor may prescribe a mild antidepressant, or even oral contraceptives in order to balance out the hormonal load in the sufferer's body. It is considered a mild condition though, as, with any type of depression, it should not be left untreated when symptoms persist.

Situational depression
Situational depression is not an official term, but it is
commonly used to refer to a condition in which a person
is afflicted by specific events or situation which may
lead them to exhibit the signs of major depression. For
instance, this could be the case of individuals who are
under a lot of stress at work, school or have been
through a traumatic experience.

Often, this may be related to PTSD and treated as such.
Other times, a doctor may diagnose it as anxiety and
prescribe therapy and counseling prior to going on
medication. The symptoms of situational depression
generally subside once the sufferer is removed from the
stressful event.

Atypical depression This type of depression may be
considered as such in individuals who don't have any
apparent cause for depression and do not exhibit the
majority of symptoms associated with major depression.
For instance, they may exhibit one, or two, symptoms
but do not show the signs of a full-blown major
depression.

As such, it is important to monitor this person's
behavior since left untreated; atypical depression may
devolve into a serious condition which may leave the
sufferer in a far worse condition than initially
anticipated. To close off this chapter, I would like to
encourage you to seek medical advice when you see that
you, or someone you care for, are exhibiting one, or

several, or these symptoms of a consistent basis. By being able to address them in time, you will be able to avoid a serious medical condition which may

require prolonged medication and therapy. By seeking help, you can take the first step toward regaining a sense of normalcy in your everyday life.

Chapter 8:

7 Worry Tricks To Crush Unwanted Anxiety, Stress And Depression

NOW THAT YOU UNDERSTAND how worry leads to anxiety, stress, and depression and have gauged your own reactions to worry and stress, it's time to get into the real nitty-gritty of this book. The following pages are going to teach you seven incredibly simple yet effective habits that will help you to stop worrying once and for all. Keep in mind that it takes 30 days to create a new habit. While these steps are simple in nature, it can still take time to put them into practice.

Don't beat yourself up about whether or not use practice all of the habits all of the time at first. This is a process, not an off switch for your worry. For this chapter, let's simply focus on the seven habits that will stop your worry and stress. In the next chapter, we will delve more deeply into how to take these seven things and use them to create lasting habits that will serve you for the rest of your life.

Habit 1: Mindfulness

BEING MINDFUL IS ABOUT being in the present moment. When you worry you are thinking about all of the things that might or might not happen. Those things, whether they are founded fears or not, are all in the future. By focusing on the present, you can put those fears to rest. Your day is made up of a series of tasks. You may be doing dishes, laundry, cooking dinner, or doing other household chores. You could be taking a shower, brushing your teeth or hair, or shaving. You could be performing any number of tasks at work or home. Even when you are doing something for relaxation such as watching television or reading a book, you are performing a task.

Being mindful means that you focus only on the task at hand. You do not allow your mind to wander to anything else. Let's say you are doing the dishes. Think about the dish in your hand. Where did you buy it? Do you have good memories of using it? How does the dish soap feel? Is the dish clean? Is something really stuck on? Keep these thoughts coming through your mind as you do the dishes. If your mind wanders to other things, consciously bring your thoughts back to the task at hand.

Being mindful will help you enjoy activities more in addition to stopping worrisome thoughts. When you focus fully on playing with your children, reading a book, or watching a movie, you more fully enjoy that activity. Mindfulness is a wonderful habit that will greatly improve your quality of life.

Habit 2: Sharing Worry

WORRYING REALLY GETS out of hand when we keep it to ourselves. It is important to voice your concerns to someone you can trust. This venting will often make you feel much better. Telling your worries to a trusted friend or family member gets them spoken out loud, where they can be more easily examined.

Your confidant may have suggestions as to why the worry is unfounded, or what else might happen as a result of what you are worrying about. You may find that you simply need an ear to listen. When you start expressing your worry to someone, you might realize just how unfounded the fears really are. You can talk

yourself through why the worry is unrealistic, and why it
should be dismissed. Sometimes all you need is a sounding board. Too often people keep their worries to themselves.

You may feel that by stating your worry out loud, you are going to make it happen. Or you might just feel that people will think you are ridiculous for worrying and judge you harshly. This is why it is important to find someone you can trust to express your worry to. This person should not be judgmental in any way. They should simply be there to listen and give input when asked for it.

They will be your voice of reason when your anxiety is too much for you to handle on your own. It is great if you have multiple people in your life who can fulfill this need. It gives you more options, and you will always know that you have someone to call regardless of the time of day. But sometimes it just takes one special person to fill this requirement.

Choose someone who you know you can trust to listen patiently and give sound advice on situations. Choose someone you know you can count on at any time that the need arises. Once you have pinpointed the best people in your life to fill this need, reach out to them and let them know what you're doing.

Tell them that you have been worrying excessively, and you no longer want to keep it to yourself. When they show understanding and are willing to help, you'll know you can count on them whenever you need to vent your worries.

Habit 3: Communication

COMMUNICATION IS EXTREMELY important for a healthy lifestyle, and even more so when you are a chronic worrier. Most people who worry a lot are just as worried about what other people are thinking as they are about events that might happen.

Don't try to be a mind reader! Accept the fact that you have no idea what is going on inside someone else's head. Speak up when you have concerns and let the other person tell you what they are thinking. For example, if you are worried that your significant other is avoiding you for some reason, voice that concern. Ask them what they have been busy with and let them know you feel neglected. Most times it is simply a lack of communication rather than a nefarious reason such as cheating.

Communication will help you in other ways as well. When you are worried, you are stressed, and when you are stressed, you may not have much patience

with others. You may find that you snap at people unnecessarily. Make the conscious effort to put a stop to this behavior. Voice your feelings. Put them out in the open. Others are better able to help you manage your anxiety, stress, and depression if they know what you are feeling. Remember, they are not mind-readers either.

Habit 4: Worst Case Scenario

IT MAY SEEM COUNTERPRODUCTIVE to imagine the worst-case scenario relating to your worry. However, this will actually help you put your worries into perspective. You will find that most of the time this exercise will help you to see how unfounded your worries are and that everything will turn out okay.

Whenever you find yourself worrying about something, ask yourself, "What is the worst thing that could reasonably happen?" The key here is that the worst-case outcome should be something reasonable. For example, if you are worried about a big project at work going wrong, think about the worst thing that could happen. You could miss the deadline. You could be reprimanded.

You could lose a bonus. Your mind will tell you that you could be fired and cause you to worry about all of the things that go along with that. But examine this fear carefully. How likely is it really that you would be fired over one project? The answer is probably not very likely. Since this is not a reasonable outcome, dismiss it. Focus on the other worst-case scenarios. You lose a bonus.

Maybe that means that you don't get to go on your camping trip or other vacation that you have planned. What is the worst-case scenario there? You stay home and do something with your significant other or family that you don't normally have time for. When you put it into perspective this way, you will quickly realize that it is not, in fact, the end of the world if things don't go as planned.

When you make that realization, you will automatically stop worrying about it. The real key here is to focus on the worst-case scenario that is *likely* to happen. For example, how likely is it that you're going to be hit by a car walking across the street crossing with the light? Pretty slim. How likely is it that you are going to die in a plane crash? About as likely as winning the lottery. Most fears are completely unfounded and recognizing that fact is going to save you a lot of stress and anxiety.

Habit 5: Meditate

MEDITATION ISN'T JUST for new agers. There is a very good reason why meditation has swept the world by storm in the last few years. It is a great way to relieve stress and stop anxiety in its tracks. Many people think that meditation is impossible for them. "I can't stop thinking, how am I supposed to meditate?" Of course, you can't stop thinking. Very few people are completely devoid of thought at any given time.

The key to meditation is to let those thoughts flow without dwelling on them. It can be helpful to have some instrumental music or nature sounds playing when you meditate. It gives you something to focus on during the meditation. There are also some great guided meditations out there on podcasts and smartphone apps that will walk you through visualizations that are very relaxing.

As you meditate, you will undoubtedly be thinking. Every time a thought comes to mind, acknowledge it, then let it go. Do not focus on any one thought or let one thought lead to another. Simply let them pass as you focus on your background music or sounds. You can also focus on your breathing, breathing deeply and rhythmically.

Meditation can be difficult to begin with, but eventually, it will become easier with practice. Once you are good at meditation, you will be able to meditate literally anywhere and at any time. You can then use these meditation techniques to stop yourself from worrying and bring you back to the present moment.

Meditation is proven to lower blood pressure and heart rate, decrease cortisol production, and increase serotonin and dopamine production. In other words, meditation directly counteracts the very effects of the worrying that you have been doing.

Habit 6: Worry Time
ESPECIALLY WHEN YOU are just starting to break the cycle of worrying, it can be difficult to just stop thinking about everything that could go wrong. Setting aside worry time is a way to remain productive and enjoy the present, while still acknowledging your fears. Essentially, you are just putting your worrying off for a future time.

Set aside time, between 30 to 60 minutes each day, that you will spend thinking about everything that is worrying you. Throughout the day when you think of something to worry about, tell yourself not now and put it aside to think about later. Train yourself to only worry during your worry time. It is a good idea to combine worry time with working out. Working out helps reduce the effects of cortisol and helps to reduce stress and anxiety. Being active can also help break cycles of depression. It is highly recommended that you create a workout routine to help combat these mental health issues.

Worry time is the perfect combination. When you are worrying, your body is releasing epinephrine and adrenaline in response to your anxiety. This will give you a burst of energy. Most people who are worrying have trouble sitting still or focusing on any one task because of this burst of energy. Why not put it to use? There are some ways you can use your worry time. You can go for a walk or jog around the neighborhood.

You can use a treadmill or exercise bike at home or at the gym. Weight lifting can also be a good workout. You don't necessarily have to do the same workout activity each day for your worry time. In fact, experts suggest that you have cardio at least three times per week and strength training twice per week for good health.

As you are working out, let your mind drift back to all of the things you were worrying about throughout the day. Think carefully about these things and remember the other habits discussed in this chapter. What is the worstcase scenario? Have you communicated your worry or fears to the people involved? Is this something you need to talk about to your therapist or your go-to worry sounding board person?

Working out is a great time to do your worrying because not only do you have the energy to spare, but it takes little thought to do most exercise activities. You can simply start exercising and just let your thoughts drift. The important thing to remember is that you should set a timer for your worry time.

When worry time is over, it's time to go back to reality and stop worrying. You will probably feel much better after your worry time. If you feel worse, try meditation or deep breathing to help you center yourself and get back to living in the present moment.

Habit 7: Change Your Beliefs
MOST CHRONIC WORRIERS have specific beliefs that lend to their worrying habit. They have worried for so

much of their lives that they feel it is completely ingrained into who they are. If this is you, you probably have some beliefs that need to be reworked. Most chronic worriers think that they have the "worry gene" and they can't help but to worry about everything. This is usually the result of growing up with a parent or grandparent who was a constant worrier.

You learned the behavior of worrying from those surrounding you as you grew up, and therefore it is ingrained into your being. Change this belief. You do not have to worry. You can change. Whenever you find yourself worrying about something unnecessarily, simply tell yourself to "Stop!" Remind yourself that worrying is not something that is inherited, and it is not something that you cannot change. It is something you have lived with for long enough, and it's time to break the cycle.

Chronic worriers also have the belief that nothing is safe. The world is an unsafe place, and therefore it is natural to worry about everything. Change this way of thinking to something more positive. If you do things that will help you and your family stay safe, that makes your world a safer place, and there is little else to worry about. For example, if you find yourself worried about a car accident, make sure that you and your family are wearing their seatbelts. It seems simple but changing this way of thinking can be somewhat difficult. It takes time and practice.

Another belief that chronic worriers face is that bad things happen in the world, and you have to always be on guard so that you can react quickly when they happen. The problem with this line of thinking is that you will constantly be waiting for something bad to happen and you will never enjoy what is happening at the moment.

Change this belief to think instead of the good things that are happening. Bad things do happen to good people but consider all of the good things that have happened and are happening to you and your family. When you turn your focus from what might happen to what is happening, you will find that the good always outweighs the bad.

Bonus Habit 8: Praise Yourself

THIS IS THE SIMPLEST habit, but it will really help you along your path to stop worrying. Whenever you follow through on one of the habits listed above, praise yourself for a job well done. The next chapter will discuss how to start

putting these habits into practice. As you complete each step and get through each day, give yourself credit where it is due. Don't focus on the times you worried, but rather focus on all of the times you didn't let it stop you.

Chapter 9:

Putting These Habits Into Practice

WHILE MOST OF THE HABITS discussed in the previous chapter seem simple enough, actually putting them into practice can be somewhat difficult. Remember that it takes 30 days to break a habit, and 30 days to create a new one.

You are doing both creating new habits and breaking an old one. It takes a certain strength and determination, as well as some careful planning. You also might find that additional research to learn coping techniques is important.

Create a Routine
HAVING A SET ROUTINE for your day is the best way to build new habits. Sit down and make a list of everything you have to do each day, and devise a schedule to get it all done. You may not have enough things to fill up the day, and that's actually a good thing. Downtime is also important.

The key here is to plan out when you will do certain activities. Schedule your meal times and stick to them to avoid the undereating or overeating that comes with stress and depression. Schedule your worry time for the same time each day. Usually, the end of the day is best. Create a workout schedule of what exercises you will do on which days of the week during your worry time.

Schedule at least three times per day when you will meditate. Then schedule time for housework, work, or other activities. When you have a set routine, it is easier to build new habits. You will do the same activity at the same time each day, and eventually, it will simply become second nature. You will feel out of balance when you don't follow your routine.

Keep in mind, however, that this is a guideline, not something set in stone. Every day is different. You may have activities come up on a specific day that are out of the norm and throw off your routine. When this happens sit down and plan out your day. Adjust your routine to accommodate that day's plans. But make sure that the important parts like your worry time stay intact. Even if you have to move the time, make sure you still fit in your worry time and meditation time.

Bedtime Rituals

A BEDTIME RITUAL IS an important part of your daily
routine. Most chronic worriers have a very difficult time
going to sleep. As your body relaxes and you settle down
to the business of sleep, all of the worries of the day can
come rushing back to you. A bedtime ritual will help
prepare your body for sleep and make it easier to fall
asleep faster. The faster you can fall asleep, the less
time your mind has to play tricks on you and drudge up
all of the worries of the day and of tomorrow.

Preparing your body for sleep is vitally important to this
process. Your bedtime ritual should start at least an
hour before you actually plan to go to bed. Start by
eliminating "screen time" before bed. The ambient light
from televisions, computers, laptops, tablets, and
smartphones tricks your brain into thinking that it's
daytime and time to be awake. Taking all of that away
an hour or two before bed will really help you fall asleep
faster. Find something to do that will allow you to relax
and wind down from the day, and then do it mindfully.
Whether it's read a book, crocheting a blanket, or
writing in your journal, make sure that all of your
attention is on that task.

Don't allow your mind to wander back to the worries of
the day. If you start feeling anxiety, your body will
produce adrenaline, and you won't be the slightest bit
sleepy. It can be a good idea to start your bedtime ritual
shortly after your worry time. This will allow you to lie in
bed with a clean slate, so to speak.

All of the worries will already be out of your system, so
you'll be better able to shut down those thoughts while
you try to go to sleep. Meditation just before bed can
also be helpful. If worrisome thoughts do try to invade

as you lay down to sleep, use your meditation skills to release them.

Do not acknowledge the thoughts. Just recognize that you have had a worry, and let it go. If you do not grab onto the worrisome thoughts and continue to think about them, they will pass, and you'll be able to fall asleep.

Use To Do Lists
IF YOUR LIFE IS ESPECIALLY hectic with work or family, having one set routine that works for every single day can be difficult. What's more, a lot of worrying happens simply because you are afraid that you're not getting everything done. Making to-do lists will help with both of these points.

You can make a to-do list at the beginning of each day. Write out everything you are worrying about getting done. Prioritize the list. What absolutely has to be done today? What can be put off? What is the worst thing that will happen if you don't accomplish this particular task? Once you have your to-do list ready for the day, you can work it into your devised routine.

You may have to adjust your routine to specific events that are time sensitive, but each day you will start with a plan of attack. Often just having the plan in place will help you ease your worrying habits. Again, keep in mind that this is always a guide. Don't let yourself get so caught up in scheduling things that it becomes another worry. You will get there. Allow yourself time to get off track, or for things to not go as planned. The important thing is to start with a plan that is flexible so that you can adjust it as necessary without added stress.

Post-It Notes YOU CAN BUY A LARGE stack of post-it notes from an office supply store for under $10. Get yourself a medium point sharpie and go to town making notes to remind yourself of your new habits. Put post-it notes in all the places you find yourself worrying the most. If you have a favorite chair in your living room, put one on the wall next to it. Put them on the bathroom mirror, on your dresser, next to your bed, and anywhere else you find yourself worrying.

The post-it notes don't have to be detailed. You can just write "Stop!" to remind yourself to stop worrying and put it off for your worry time. Put a post-it on the phone to remind yourself to call your go-to sounding board person and vent your worries when necessary. Put a post it in the car to remind yourself that worries are unfounded, and you will make it home safely. You can also put post-it notes up at work. Again, you can have a note that simply says "stop" or "wait" to remind yourself to put your worry off for later. The note could say "now" to remind yourself to be mindful and remain in the present.

Don't be self-conscious about the post-it notes. There is no reason to feel ashamed for using them, and you have no need to explain them to anyone. You can write whatever will help you build on the seven habits discussed in the previous chapter, and they do not have to shout to the world that you are trying to stop worrying.

A simple note that says "now" or "stop" could be explained some ways, if an explanation were even to become necessary. If you're really self-conscious about having post-it notes up in a certain place, scour the internet for good signs and memes that will help you build your new habits and stop worrying of them. You can purchase wood or metal signs for your home that will just look like part of the regular décor. Or you could print out memes and post them in your home or office in picture frames.

The goal of the post-it notes or signs is to keep your goals to the forefront of your mind constantly. It reinforces your new habits by keeping them fresh. You will find that eventually, you don't look at them anymore, and you can take them down. Or, you could leave them up as a reminder of how far you've come.

Make Time for Communication

WHEN YOU ARE DEVELOPING your routine, or just throughout each day, make time to communicate with those around you. If you find yourself worrying about something at work, make time to talk it over with a co-worker or your boss. Make time especially for a conversation with your spouse or significant other, and your children if they are older. Making time for communication will help you implement the habit of voicing your thoughts and actually knowing what others are thinking.

Opening up the lines of communication thoughtfully and purposefully will not only stop your worrying, but it will also improve your relationships. You will find that it becomes much easier to put your fears aside when you are able to communicate them to others.

Look Up Statistics

WHEN DEVELOPING THE habit of considering the worst-case scenario, it can be helpful to look up statistics on things you are worrying about. How likely is it really that you will be in a car accident or a plane crash? How likely is it that your spouse is cheating? How likely is it that you will have to find another job at your age, and if that were to happen, how likely is it you will easily find another one?

Anything that has you worrying likely has a statistic to match. You will be amazed at how slim the odds really are of bad things happening to you and your loved ones. The very act of looking up the statistics on a certain fear will put your mind at ease and allow you to think of other things. Once you've looked it up, you can remind yourself of the facts whenever the worry crops back up, as it undoubtedly will until you break the habit.

Guided Meditation

MEDITATION SEEMS LIKE it should be easy, but for many people, it is actually a difficult skill to develop. Until you are proficient at meditation, it can be helpful to use guided meditations to help you learn the habit. Prepare for your meditation practice ahead of time by looking up podcasts, YouTube videos and smartphone apps that provide guided meditations. There are a lot of them out there, and you can pick and choose the ones that you think will work best for you.

When you are sifting through the masses, make sure you choose some of different lengths. Thirty-minute guided meditations are great for your scheduled meditation practice as a part of your daily routine that you should have devised. Shorter five-minute meditations are better for those times when you really just need a time out from your worrying and stress. You might also want to look up and download or create a playlist of some music that is soothing and suitable for meditation. This will be instrumental music of some type. It can be piano music, waltzes, ballet music, or classical music.

There are a lot of instrumental tracks out there as well for meditation that include nature sounds with the instrumental music as a backdrop. Nature sounds on their own can also be used for meditation.

Let Your New Routine Be Known

MAKE SURE THAT YOU talk to your spouse or significant other and your children, as well as anyone else you live with or see daily. Hold a family meeting if you need to. Let everyone know about your new routine, and especially about your designated worry time. Even younger children can understand that you have a specific time set aside for yourself that they are not to interrupt unless necessary.

This prepares the way for you to be able to have your meditation and worry time uninterrupted. It will be much easier to build these habits if you can stick to your routine, and it will be easier to stick to your routine if everyone is on board. It is especially important that everyone in your household knows when to leave you to your worry time.

If you are single and have roommates, you don't have to talk to them about what the time is for. Just let them know that during this set time every day you are to be left undisturbed. You might also get a do not disturb sign for your door to help keep out unwanted distractions during your meditations.

Be Easy On Yourself

REMEMBER THAT CHANGE does not happen overnight. It takes time to build new habits and break old ones. It takes trial and error. Something that you think will work for you might turn out to be harmful or indifferent rather than helpful. Remember that this is a new process for you, and you never know how things will go. Just because you have planned out a routine and use to-do lists doesn't mean everything will always go as planned. Learn to roll with the punches.

Don't let it stop you from making positive changes. Most of all, do not beat yourself up when it doesn't work right away. These things take time. If you find yourself worrying excessively about something after starting these new habits, it's not a reflection on you as a person. Know that you are trying to make the changes, and they will come eventually. Have patience with yourself.

Chapter 10:

Why Self Care and Self Love is Important

THROUGHOUT THIS BOOK, you have heard the theme that you have to be easy on yourself through this process. This chapter is going to delve deeper into why this is so important. You must have patience with yourself and care for yourself in other ways, or the process will not abate your stress and depression.

You have to take care of yourself, physically, mentally and emotionally. You have to give yourself time to pamper yourself and schedule in some downtime. A lot of chronic worriers also worry about taking time for themselves away from family. You absolutely must do this without guilt.

You Can't Run on Empty

YOU LIKELY HAVE HEARD the phrase "you can't pour from an empty cup." You'll never realize how true this is until you hit bottom. When your anxiety, stress, and depression overwhelm you, you have no energy. You have no desire to do anything. You feel like giving up. And you can't give to your employer or your family if you are running on empty.

Do things to replenish your spirit. Take a bubble bath with some soothing music playing in the background. Hide in your bedroom with a good book for an hour before dinner or while the children are napping. Don't take your lunch break in your office but go out for a walk or eat your lunch under the trees in a park. There is a number of things that you can do to give yourself downtime throughout your day, regardless of your lifestyle. Think about things that you enjoy, and things that are relaxing to you. Make a list of those things, and how long you might need to do them.

Then, find ways to work them into your daily routine. It's also okay to need downtime on the spur of the moment. Never feel guilty about needing to replenish your own energy. Take time to ground yourself and prepare for facing the rest of the day. Even if all you do is go to the restroom and practice deep breathing for five minutes, that self-care will help you get through the day, mood intact.

You have Purpose

YOU HAVE A PURPOSE in this life. If you are a parent, finding your purpose is easy. You have to be a good role model and teacher for your children. If you have yet to have a family of your own, find purpose in other areas of your life. You can volunteer or support a cause that means a lot to you.

Everyone has a purpose. You just have to find it and exploit it. Often people with depression feel that they have no purpose in this life. They feel they are drifting, and not contributing anything to the world. Do not allow yourself to fall into this trap. Knowing that you have a purpose will help pull you out of your depression.

Having purpose will also help you meet your goals and build these new worry-free habits. You cannot fulfill your purpose if you are always worrying. Use your new-found purpose to fuel your desires to make these positive changes in your life. If you ever find yourself doubting that you have a purpose, do some journaling to discover ways you have made a difference and ways you can continue

to do so in the future. Everyone has made a difference in the life of others in some way. Find the ways you make a difference. If you need to, talk to a trusted friend or therapist to help you discover your purpose.

Self-Doubt Fuels Depression
REMEMBER THAT YOU ARE working to break a cycle. Worry leads to anxiety, which leads to stress, which leads to depression. Self-doubt fuels that depression; like jet fuel to an engine. Every time you doubt yourself and your ability to make these changes, you are fueling your depression.

This is just going to lead to more worrying about how you are going to break the cycle, and whether or not you are meeting your other obligations. You have to have faith in yourself and your ability to make positive changes. Any time you find yourself doubting yourself, think about times that you have overcome obstacles. Think about positive changes you have already made in your life.

Make a list of successes and celebrate them. Journaling is a great tool for this. When you chronicle your successes, you can look back on them and reflect during the times that you feel less than worthy.

Self-Love Makes All Things Possible
SELF-LOVE BUILDS Self-confidence and gives you the strength to face obstacles. When you truly love yourself, in spite of your flaws, you find the strength to face the world through adversity. This will not only improve your mental health, but it will actually decrease the number of things that you worry about. Think about it this way. Your spouse is not perfect. Your parents are not perfect.

Your children are not perfect. No one is. But you love them anyway, unconditionally.

You love them even when they make mistakes, even when they hurt you or others. You have to put that into practice for yourself. Give yourself permission to love yourself unconditionally. Know that you are a worthy person, worthy of love from others and from yourself. Everyone has flaws, but they don't make you any less lovable. Self-love can be difficult if you are a perfectionist, or if you have had people in your life who have told you that you are not worthy of love.

It is important to conquer those fears and know that you are worthy of self-love, and you are capable of it. When you have a love for yourself, all things become possible. Because you love yourself unconditionally and can trust that when things go wrong, you will still be a strong, confident person, all obstacles will seem surmountable. The possibilities are truly endless when you stop doubting and love yourself completely.

Have Patience

PATIENCE IS A VIRTUE, and it is a sad fact that most chronic worriers don't have it naturally. Sometimes our worries are directly related to a lack of patience. We worry that things are not happening fast enough, or that something that should be happening isn't on the schedule.

Remember that this is a process. It takes time to build up new habits and break old ones. Change doesn't happen overnight. It doesn't matter how committed you are to making the change, it will take time. You have to have patience with yourself above all else. You are going to have setbacks. You are going to have times when the worrying just won't go away, no matter what you do. This is going to continue to happen until your new habits are firmly in place. And it's okay.

Recognize that No One is Perfect

A LOT OF CHRONIC WORRIERS are perfectionists. You worry because things are not perfect. You worry because you are not perfect, or your family isn't perfect. Well here's the truth of it: No one and no thing is perfect in every way.

Recent studies show that perfectionism leads to poor quality of life, poor mental health, and poor physical health. Perfectionists worry so much about being perfect that they don't enjoy life. They constantly feel that they are not good enough, leading to anxiety and depression. It also causes stress, which leads to its own physical health concerns. Embrace the fact that you are not perfect. If everyone were perfect, everyone would be the same, and that would make life very boring indeed. Embrace your flaws.

Acknowledge that sometimes you are just going to have a bad day. Acknowledge that sometimes, you're going to revert back to worrying about something. And acknowledge that this is perfectly okay to be imperfect.

Self-Talk

HOW TO TALK TO YOURSELF and about yourself directly affects your ability to pull out of depression and make changes to better your life. A prime example of poor self-talk is constantly apologizing to yourself and others, even when no apology is really necessary. You may find yourself telling yourself or others that you have failed in some way, or that you aren't strong enough to make changes.

You have to work hard to battle this negative self-talk. Anytime you catch yourself apologizing to yourself or someone else for something beyond your control, stop yourself. Vocally, out loud, state why the apology was unnecessary. If you are in conversation with someone else, they will likely agree with you, and you can move on.

Daily affirmations are a great way to battle negative self-talk. Some people think that daily affirmations seem silly. It can seem a bit awkward to talk to yourself in the mirror. Saturday Night Live skits have done little to make daily affirmations commonplace, often making them the butt of jokes.

Try to put all of those feelings aside. Remember, no one has to hear you or see you do these affirmations. Stand in front of the mirror in your bedroom or in the bathroom. Saying them out loud is great, but if you're worried someone will overhear you can talk to yourself silently. After all, the words are for you, and you alone.

You can use daily affirmations in the morning when you get up or at night when you go to bed. You can use them throughout the day any time you catch yourself in self-doubt or harmful self-talk. Here are some examples:

"I am strong willed and will overcome these obstacles."

"I will not let worry and fear control me."

"I am stronger than my fear."

"I am a warrior, not a worrier."

"All is well.

Nothing bad is happening. I am okay."

"I matter."

"I am worthy."

"I am making progress."

"I can control my thoughts and actions."

"I am good enough. I have purpose."

You can use any of these affirmations or create your own. There are also books and calendars that you can buy with daily affirmations. The important thing about this is to make it about traits you have or want to have.

Make the affirmations about what is good about you. The idea is to promote self-love in whatever way will help you keep going.

Chapter 11:

Alternative Remedies to Overcome Depression

Throughout this book, we have discussed the treatment options for anxiety and depression. As indicated earlier, depression tends to be almost always treated with a course in medication. Prescription drugs generally treat the chemical reactions in the brain which cause the majority of symptoms associated with depression.

The worst thing that can happen to someone who is battling with depression, in particular, is to find themselves alone and uncared for. When this happens, the feelings of despair and despondency will only heighten. This may lead to suicidal thoughts and even to acting upon them.

You can help others battling with these conditions by providing them with a safe and loving environment in which they can be themselves. This is especially important for children and teenagers. Feeling comforted and cared for has a powerful effect to alleviate any of the symptoms we have previously described.

This point ties into showing sufferers how much you care about them. Perhaps you may not fully understand what they are going through, but you may be able to understand that they need help and support.

Now, this can be challenging especially when the sufferer is in denial and doesn't believe they actually need any help. In such cases, you may be met with resistance and even rejection. Often, anxiety and depression sufferers aren't aware of what's wrong and may feel offended that you are bringing up the subject.

Then, there are those who are suffering in silence. These individuals may be crying out for help in subtle ways. So, it's up to you to pick up on those and just offer and friendly smile and a shoulder to lean on. When you have become aware that a person may be in a severe depression, then the time to act may be very short. When sufferers fall into severe depression, they may be inclined to act upon the negative thoughts they get. By this time, it may be too late to do anything about it.

Nevertheless, you can act quickly and seek medical attention for your loved one. This may include checking them into a rehab facility or even taking a trip down to the emergency room. Whatever the case, you need to act quickly. In doing so, you can ensure the health and safety of your loved ones.

Another vital element in helping sufferers cope with their condition is education. You can help them learn more about their condition, what triggers it and how they can find ways to cope with it. Bear in mind that someone in the grasp of severe anxiety and depression may not be able to fully think for themselves.

This is where your support is vital in helping them understand the options available to them and what may be the best course of action. This may include medication or natural home remedies. In the event that you, yourself, have been through this path yourself, you have valuable experience which you can share with others who are suffering just like you once did. I have found it useful to acquaint myself with others who have been through the same experiences as I have.

These similar experiences have allowed me to develop a deeper understanding of what anxiety and depression are, and how to cope with them. You may choose to engage in counseling, support therapy groups or just lend a friendly ear to anyone who is need of a friend. In doing so, you are helping others learn to cope with their condition and become self-sufficient. So, I would encourage you to find out which organization support anxiety and depression sufferers in your local communities.

Often, these organizations are part of larger health associations, churches, or volunteer groups. Nowadays, most schools offer counseling programs for kids and teens. They not only teach kids how to deal with what they are currently feeling, but also provide a proactive approach so that these conditions do not develop in younger generations. I am certain that kids and teens would be interested to hear your experience as they may be struggling with something similar themselves.

Finally, helping others cope with their struggles is not an easy task as it can be emotionally draining. I have often felt helpless when trying to reach people who simply do not want to listen. While you may have all the good intentions in the world, these folks just need time and space before they can react to your supportive efforts. Of course, the only time I would agree with your acting in spite of someone's resistance is when it is clear they are a danger to others and themselves.

This is especially important with members of your family or very close friends. You can bring their family on board and get them the help they need. In the event that the family of a sufferer is unwilling to get someone the help they need, you can contact a local social worker or healthcare professional who can assist you in finding the proper channels to get depressed individuals the help they need.

This can be especially challenging when underage children and teenagers are being neglected the help they need. At the end of the day, it pays to do your homework before attempting to help others.

Do your research online, read books such as this one, take classes, attend seminars; do whatever you can to improve your knowledge base as this will help you gain more insight as to what you can do to help others find the right path toward regaining a balanced life. Bear in mind that this is no easy task. But your dedication and efforts in helping others will contribute greatly toward ensuring the health and wellbeing of those who are struggling to cope with debilitating conditions such as anxiety and depression.

In addition, counseling and therapy are also prescribed in order to help sufferers get a better handle on their symptoms and what they can do in order to improve their overall outlook on life and the condition they are dealing with. In this chapter, we will be looking at three ways in which you can utilize home remedies to help deal with symptoms of depression. It should be noted that these remedies, by no means, should replace the treatment provided by a healthcare professional. Nevertheless, these remedies can be used in tandem to help the sufferer deal with the symptoms associated with depression, especially in a proactive manner.

Massage therapy

When you think of massages, what comes to mind? Exactly! Relaxation. Massage therapy is a great way of alleviating the onset of negative feelings associated with depression. As such, it is important for the sufferer to be aware of the onset of these feelings in order to seek help. This type of therapy can be done in tandem or even alone by massage and stimulating certain pressure points such as the soles of your feet. In essence, massage therapy can be something as simple as a shoulder or foot rub when feelings begin to manifest themselves, or it can be a full-body massage.

This is where I have indicated that massage therapy can be used as a proactive approach. How so? Well, the sufferer may choose to attend regular massage sessions in which the massage therapist may focus on specific parts of the body, or just do a fullbody massage. Either way, the massage therapist should be aware of the reason for the massage so that they may take this consideration into mind.

In addition, sufferers may seek back adjustments in order to alleviate pain which may also be derived from bad posture or pain derived from muscle spasms resulting from large amounts of stress and anxiety. Massage treatment should be discussed with your doctor beforehand in order to understand and agree on the best options available to the sufferer and maximize the benefit derived from this type of treatment.

Herbal supplements
Herbal supplements, such as St. John's Wort, are widely believed to help with symptoms of depression though there is no conclusive scientific evidence supporting this notion. That is not to say that the consumption of herbal supplements is not recommended or ineffective. What that means is that herbal supplements may end up doing little to actually help the sufferer's condition.

This is why you must talk to your doctor first prior to taking any herbal supplements. Of course, herbal supplements rarely cause any type of interaction with traditional medication, but it is worth discussing as your doctor should be aware of any such decisions. Now, taking herbal supplements as a proactive approach especially when you are not on medication may prove to be a viable option especially when you are going through prolonged periods of stress due to a high-stress job, school, or any other situation which may lead you to show some signs of depression like symptoms. Another herbal supplement which is widely believed to help reduce feelings of anxiety and promote good sleep is Valerian Root.

This supplement is readily available and can be taken regularly when a person finds themselves in a stressful situation or may be having trouble sleeping. In addition, it is believed to help promote overall wellness in depression sufferers. As with St. John's Wort, you should discuss this supplementation with your doctor if you are on medication. If you are not under medication, then this supplement could be used to help you relax and unwind at the end of a stressful day.

Other indications for this supplement are that it may be taken throughout the day especially during stressful situations. I would advise you to take it at home first and see how your body reacts. That way, if you choose to take it at work or school, you can be ready for the reaction this will have on your body.

Don't forget about yoga
The last home remedy I would like to recommend is yoga. Yoga and meditation generally go hand in hand, though meditation is generally a mental and emotional exercise while yoga is a purely physical exercise.

When you do yoga, the positions require you to focus your mind and body on how you need to mold your body in order to achieve such positions. This tends to take the mind away from the causes of stress, and negative thoughts, and focus on the exercises being done. Some folks feel that yoga is better done in a group rather than alone.

This could be a great way of finding a balance especially if you suffer from social anxiety. Also, yoga is a great way to start off the day on a positive note. 30 to 45 minutes of yoga exercises can help you feel relaxed and much more comfortable with yourself and your surroundings. Therapists often prescribe yoga due to its relaxation effects on anxiety sufferers.

For depression sufferers, yoga can be a great way to get some exercise in without even having to leave the house.

So, it is definitely an option worth looking into. There are plenty of yoga tutorials online.

As such, you can do these routines from the comfort of your own home. Yoga, combined with mindfulness and meditation, will help you connect with yourself at a much deeper level. Consequently, you will be able to find a balance between yourself and a deeper consciousness that surrounds. I highly encourage you to give yoga a try. It is one of the few exercises that provides both physical and mental practice.

Chapter 12:

Alternative Remedies to Overcome Anxiety

In the previous chapter, we looked at a series of remedies which you can put to use at home in order to help you overcome anxiety and feelings of sadness, along with physical symptoms. In this chapter, we will be focusing on remedies which can help you deal with anxiety. While depression is a clinical condition that often requires medical attention in addition to medication, anxiety sufferers may not be at a point where they need medication; they just need to find the right balance in order to ensure that they are able to cope with the stress in their lives.

As such, this chapter focuses on what to do, as well as, what not to do. Therefore, it's worth keeping an eye on the remedies which you can put to use in order to help you regain a balance in your day-to-day life.

Ditch caffeine, cigarettes, alcohol, and sugar
In general, anxiety has its roots in psychological and emotional imbalances. When this happens, you may find yourself falling prey to large amounts of stress that come with specific jobs and careers or simply having to live with negative situations such as the death of a loved one, illness, financial distress among other stressful situation.

When this occurs, folks tend to resort to substance abuse as a coping mechanism. Substances abuse can be as mild as overdoing coffee while getting into more serious situations such as the consumption of narcotics and prescription drugs.

Thus, one of the first things I would encourage you to do is to look at your diet and see which elements may be fueling your anxiety. For instance, if you are consuming large amounts of alcohol, you could be predisposing yourself for anxiety.

Also, having a healthy and balanced diet is one of the best things you can do in order to ensure that you are not setting yourself up for further anxiety attacks. In particular, high sugar consumption can put you on edge.

As a matter of fact, one rather common cause of anxiety is withdrawal-like symptoms when folks consume a lesser amount than they are accustomed to a particular substance. For example, drinking less coffee than usual may trigger an anxiety attack. The same goes for sugar and cigarettes.

In the case of alcohol and narcotics, the withdrawal-type symptoms may be so severe that medical intervention may be required in order to stabilize the sufferer. In which case, on common course of action is to seek a rehab facility which specializes in treating anxiety derived from substance abuse.

However, if you just drink too much coffee, maybe have a bit too many sweets and may overdo alcohol once in a while, it would certainly be worth having you cut down significantly on it. Ideally, you would eliminate the consumption of these substances, but that may not always be possible. However, if you feel that you would be unable to get such a habit under control, then it would be best to seek medical attention and rid yourself of these potentially harmful substances.

Stock up on tea
Tea is a great home remedy which you can use to help you curb your anxiety. While it is true that black tea contains caffeine, there are a host of herbal teas which do not — as such, drinking tea may be a perfect alternative to drinking coffee especially if you can't wrap your mind around switching to decaf.

Herbal teas such as green tea are packed with antioxidants which can help your body rid itself of toxic substances while providing you with elements to help fight off high blood pressure and even clear your liver of unwanted substances.

Other teas such as chamomile, peppermint, and lemon are tasty alternatives to regular black and green tea. Chamomile has anti-inflammatory properties which can help reduce overall inflammation in the body while helping you calm down especially after a stressful day.

Peppermint and lemon teas have been found to not only contain antioxidants but have also been widely used as a soothing agent especially after stressful and traumatic events. Since both peppermint and lemon are loaded with antioxidants and flavonoids, they make for ideal choices when looking to calm down and unwind.

Also, you can drink them throughout the day and serve as an excellent alternative to coffee. Finally, teas such as Gotu Kola and Valerian, when consumed regularly, may prove to be as beneficial as taking as herbal supplement or even consuming mild antidepressants.

Naturally, the key here is to be consistent in your tea consumption.

Prayer

Earlier, we talked about having a closer relationship with a higher power. Regardless of whichever faith you may profess, being close to a higher power is an absolute need for all humans.

We all need to engage our spiritual selves in such a way that we able to connect with a deeper, more profound part of ourselves. This is where prayer can help you not only connect with that deeper part of yourself, but also help relieve those feelings of anguish which may attack you from time to time. I have found that regular prayer is a great way to help relieve feelings of uneasiness and uncertainty. Now, there aren't any specific prayers or mantras here. You can take your holy book and find a passage which is especially comforting, or you can recite prayers which are specific to your faith.

I would also encourage you to speak with your spiritual guide so that they may provide you with some ways you can engage your faith further. I have known folks who find peace and solace at their local church while others find calm in prayer groups.

Therefore, engaging in regular prayer and worship are two simple but effective elements which you can do in the comfort of your home or a part of a larger community. In addition, that feeling of belonging to a larger community will help you feel at ease since you can be sure that there are others who care about you and wish you nothing but the best.

Conclusion

Well, we have come to the end of this incredible path. It seems unbelievable that we have covered so much in such a short period of time. In this book, we have gone over anxiety and depression, their causes and the ways in which you, or someone you care for, can deal with them through natural tricks.

We have established how medical attention is essential in helping anxiety and depression sufferer cope with the condition they are facing. Often, sufferers are perfectly willing to receive help though they may not even know where to begin. This is why understanding treatment options are essential in helping sufferers overcome their feelings.

The most important thing to bear in mind is that the safety and wellbeing of the sufferer is the main thing to keep in mind. This is why recognizing even the subtlest signs of trouble may serve to help a person who is suffering, especially those who are suffering in silence. This is why education is the first step. With proper education, you can learn about ways in which you can help others deal with this condition.

The most important thing to keep in mind is that sufferers are not alone. Depression, in particular, can heighten feelings of abandonment and rejection. So, being able to help sufferers by lending a helping hand is as powerful as tactic as any medication.

Ultimately, I would encourage you to consult your doctor especially before trying out home remedies and other alternative therapies. This is especially important if you are taking medication as potential interactions with other medications may have adverse effects. Also, it pays to look into groups and organizations which you can count on to provide you with support and attention when needed. By being part of a support group, you can find a great source of moral support.

In addition, there are great therapy and counseling programs which are run by volunteers. Often, these are folks who have been through the same situation you are currently going through. As such, they can offer help and insights which are relevant to those who have dealt with similar conditions.

And so, I would like to thank you for reading this book. I hope you have found it useful and informative. Above all, I hope that you have found ways in which you can help yourself, and those whom you know may be struggling with this condition. Please bear in mind that depression and anxiety are not a sign of weakness.

After all, would you label a cancer patient as being weak? The same goes for anxiety and depression sufferers. Anxiety and depression sufferers are regular folks who are simply going through a rough patch. This is why helping sufferers feel that these conditions are not worthy of stigma or shame is a vital step toward helping them seek the help they need in order to enter the path to recovery. I would also like to thank you for showing concern for someone whom you know may be going through this situation. I hope you have found answers to your questions though I would encourage you to further your study and understanding of these conditions and how you can utilize the many options which are available to you. If you are struggling with these conditions, then I hope you have also found answers to your questions herein. I would also encourage you to ask for help. Even if you are alone, you can seek folks who can provide you with help and attention in order to get back on track. You have already taken the first step on your road to recovery.